British Pavilion
Seville Exposition 1992

Phaidon Press Ltd
140 Kensington Church Street
London W8 4BN

First published 1992
Reprinted 1993
© 1992, Phaidon Press Limited
Photographs © 1992, Jo Reid
& John Peck except where
stated to the contrary

ISBN 0 7148 2747 9

A CIP catalogue record for this
book is available from the British
Library

Design: Mark Vernon-Jones

Printed and bound in Hong Kong

Photographs 36, 37, 39, 40 and
those on pages 4 (top) and 23
are by John Edward Linden.
Photographs 1, 2, 3, 4, 5 and 6
are courtesy of the *Architects'
Journal* photographic library.

**British Pavilion
Seville Exposition 1992**
Nicholas Grimshaw
and Partners

COLIN DAVIES

The image of discovery;
looking north-east across the
Lake of Spain at the heart of the
Expo 92 site.

1

2

Expo 92 will be the last major international exposition of the 20th century, the century which has seen Western industrial culture spread to encompass the planet. At the height of the flowering of this culture, in the middle years of the century, it seemed that the science and technology upon which it was based had the power to solve the world's problems. Now we are not so sure. We are more aware of the damage it causes than the benefits it brings. The gap between rich and poor has increased, not diminished, and the growth cycle of production and consumption is threatening the natural environment on which it ultimately depends. Expo 92 celebrates the 500th anniversary of the 'discovery' of the Americas by Christopher Columbus – the first major advance in that global conquest. Its site is the Island of La Cartuja in the Andalucian Capital of Seville, the place from which Columbus set out on his journey. There are more than one hundred national pavilions, as well as theme pavilions, an artificial lake, a monorail, a cable car link to the city centre, an observation tower – all the traditional trappings of an International Expo. Beyond the site itself, the infrastructure of Seville and Andalucia has been improved, with a new airport, a new railway station, new motorways, and seven new bridges over the Guadalquivir River. The official theme of the Expo is Discovery, but in this troubled age, the unofficial theme is inevitably the relationship between man and his natural environment.

Ever since Joseph Paxton designed the Crystal Palace, **1**, for the Great Exhibition of 1851, International Expos have been occasions for experiments in architecture. One thinks of Le Corbusier's Pavillon de L'Esprit Nouveau, **2**, at the Paris Exposition des Arts Decoratifs of 1925, the Skylon, **3**, and the Dome of Discovery at the 1951 Festival of Britain, Buckminster Fuller's geodesic dome at Expo 67 in Montreal, **4**, and Frei Otto's cable net structure at the same Expo, **5**. When the Department of Trade and Industry ran a competition for the design of the British Pavilion, all three short-listed architects produced experimental, rather than traditional designs, and all three decided to tackle the unofficial theme of the relationship between man and his natural environment. In the hot climate of Seville, one obvious aspect of that theme presented itself: how to create comfortably cool conditions for visitors without squandering energy and creating pollution.

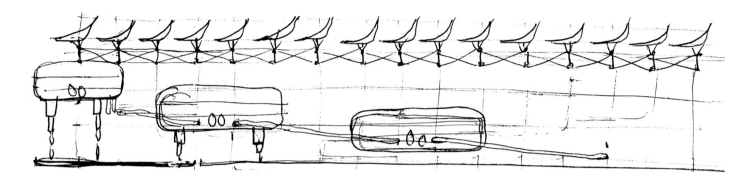

Details from Nicholas Grimshaw's sketchbooks, dated 14 January 1989, showing the initial stages of the building's sectional development.

Spence and Webster's presentation summed up the theme in the phrase 'Man's new dialogue with nature'. They designed a simple, tunnel-like enclosure with gently curved 'lamella' arches and an external envelope that would respond 'like a living organism' to changing weather conditions, **6**. Instead of conventional, high-energy consuming air-conditioning, they proposed to moderate the internal conditions by a combination of automatic variable sun control louvres, solar power cells and heat pumps. Cool air was to be circulated around the building not by ducts but by the natural 'coanda' effect, clinging to the curved surface of the fabric enclosure.

Alsop and Lyall also described their more expressive design as 'a living creature', **7**. An 'audio visual drome' shaped like the leading edge of an aeroplane wing was to be fully enclosed and air-conditioned, but the design also proposed cooling by natural means. The entrance courtyard beneath the building was to be cooled by water flowing along an internal canal, and the main glass-floored gallery space above was to be shaded by an airship that could float out through the hinged roof to hover above the building. These non air-conditioned spaces were to be transitional, temperate spaces between the sweltering heat outside and the cool of the audio visual drome.

But it was the design by Nicholas Grimshaw and Partners that marshalled these various passive climate-moderating features in the most consistent and practical way. This was the design that won the competition and which now represents Britain on the La Cartuja site.

Architect's intentions

Every piece of architecture, no matter how abstract or functional, conveys a cultural message of some kind. The conveyance of the message might be incidental to the architect's main intentions, or it might be an important part of the social function of the building. In the case of a national pavilion for an international expo the cultural message is central to the building's functional programme. When Nicholas Grimshaw set about defining the parameters of his design for the British Pavilion at Seville, he began by deciding what the building should mean, what it should represent.

The report which accompanied the competition submission listed ten concepts that the design should

6

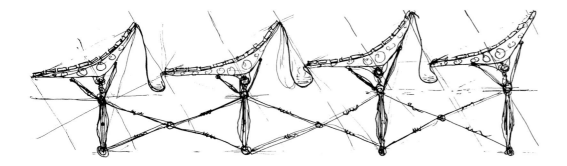

embody. These can be sorted under three main headings. First, Grimshaw decided, the building should 'express the Spirit of the Age'. This, of course is a concept that has been fundamental to the ideology of Modernist architecture every since its pioneering days in the early years of this century. For all modernist architects, but especially for those mainly British architects, including Nicholas Grimshaw, to whom the label 'high-tech' is often applied, the spirit of the modern age resides in advanced technology. For these architects, architecture has a duty to participate in, make use of and give expression to, advanced technology – the technology of industry, transport, communication, flight and space travel.

This, then, was the first and most important message to be conveyed in the design of the pavilion. It would be made from characteristically modern materials like steel, glass and plastic, and it would be assembled using the techniques of industrial production rather than traditional crafts like carpentry or masonry. It would also give frank expression to these materials and techniques, with no applied decoration or fake finishes, and it would not resort to any of the 'historicist' architectural motifs that in recent years

have reappeared on the façades and in the interiors of many new buildings in Britain and America. This would not be a classical building, or a gothic building, or a vernacular building; it would be a modern building. Most importantly, its message would not be trivial or childish, like a Disneyworld fantasy, but essentially serious, engaging real practical problems.

But now a new element has been added to the basic modernist proposition. The realization in the early 1970s that the Earth's resources, especially its energy resources, were finite and were rapidly being used up, has given way to an increasing concern, verging on panic, about the effect on the natural environment of industrial pollution. The construction and maintenance of buildings accounts for a large proportion of this global pollution. For architects who seek to celebrate industrial technology in the design of their buildings this obviously presents a problem. Some have responded by proposing a break with the twentieth century modernist tradition and a return to an architecture crafted from local, natural materials. Nicholas Grimshaw, however, maintains his faith in the human benefits that high technology has to offer. His architecture is practical and

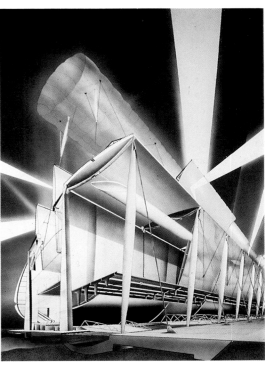

functional and for him pollution and the husbanding of global resources are problems that can only be solved scientifically by the application of modern technology.

This brings us to the second message to be conveyed in the design of the pavilion. It would be unashamedly modern, and it would be a product of industrial technology, but it would also be a demonstration of the application of that technology to the global problems of the twenty-first century. Energy conservation and the recycling of building components would be major themes. The pavilion would demonstrate how a building assembled from lightweight, factory-made components could create a place of coolness and rest in the hot climate of Seville without relying solely on an energy-wasting mechanical plant. To achieve this, it would take lessons from the local building vernacular, but apply them in an analytical and scientific way.

This was to be a national pavilion and it therefore had to say something about Britain; its people, its culture, its industry and its commerce. As well as the Spirit of the Age, it also had to express the Spirit of Britain, **8**. In the competition report the Spirit of Britain was illustrated by a picture of a Concorde airliner. Concorde was, of course, an Anglo-

French project, so the image neatly encapsulated the idea of Britain's co-operation with its European partners. This third message would be conveyed as much by the building itself as by the displays inside. A building conceived as a kit of prefabricated parts would serve this purpose very well, since the components could be made by British firms in British factories and then shipped to the site for assembly. Each component would be an exhibit as well as a functioning part of the building.

These then were the messages to be conveyed by the building itself. But what would the building contain? Having entered this British-made, high-tech haven of coolness and rest, what would the estimated 12 000 visitors per day actually see? Grimshaw's competition entry proposed that the exhibits should be interpretations of a unifying theme: water. This simple theme could be used as vehicle for all sorts of sub-themes illustrating different aspects of British culture and industry, from ship building to fish farming, from wave power to the human body (95% water), from the Channel Tunnel to Scotch Whisky. In the event, the Department of Trade and Industry rejected this idea, dividing the design responsibility between the interior

12

13

11

displays and the building that would contain them. But water nevertheless remains a central theme in Grimshaw's building, **9**. Visitors walk over a moat and through a wall of water to enter the building, and once inside, they feel the cooling effect of the thousands of gallons of water that fill containers forming the west wall, **10**.

Organization of spaces

The basic form of the building would have to reconcile several conflicting requirements. Grimshaw decided that visitors should not be forced onto a single circulation route taking them past each exhibit in turn, whether they wanted to see it or not. There must be variety and choice. For those who wanted just a quick survey of what the pavilion had to offer, movement through the building must be quick and easy, with no queueing. But there must also be opportunities to step off the route, to sit down and watch a live performance or an audio visual display, to take refreshment, or simply to linger and shelter from the heat. There must also be a variety of spatial experiences. The prominent site, at the head of the main Expo route known as EC Avenue, suggested a simple unified form, rather than a collection of smaller structures, and since the building would be an important exhibit in itself, its unity ought to be experienced internally, as well as externally. But how could this be reconciled with the functional requirement for enclosed spaces with more controlled environments?

The answer was to design these spaces as freestanding 'pods' within a simple enclosing envelope. The first proposal was for three pods set step-wise at different levels so that their roofs formed platforms from which to view the cathedral-like interior. Circulation between the pods and platforms would be via a system of bridges and ramped travelators, giving visitors (the disabled as well as the able-bodied) a choice of routes through the building, **11**. This arrangement has been modified in the final building, which has only two pods, one at each end and both at the top level.

Between them the same basic structure forms a platform supporting the funnel-shaped structure which is the focal point of the internal display, **12**, **13**. The roof of the southern pod forms the floor of an enclosure used as a VIP suite. Nevertheless the original buildings-within-a-building idea survives.

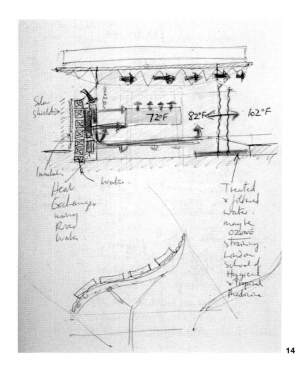

14

Energy conservation strategy

The buildings within a building idea is more than just a way to preserve the impressive unity of the interior. It is also a clear architectural expression of the energy conservation strategy of the building. The air within the main envelope is cooled by mainly passive means, with full air-conditioning limited to the interiors of the pods and the semi-basement spaces beneath the main concourse. Thus there is a gentle progression from the sweltering heat outside to the cool interiors of the pods, via the temperate zone of the main envelope, 14. Passive cooling is achieved in three ways: by running water, by external shading, and by high thermal capacity. Each face of the basically box-like form uses a different cooling device according to its orientation, 15.

The most impressive of these devices is the 'water wall' of the east façade. A sheer glass curtain wall, with no projecting mullions or transoms, supports a continuous sheet of water falling into a pool, half inside and half outside the building, 16. Visitors cross this pool on a ramped steel bridge and enter the building through an opening in the water wall. The water is pumped from the pool to the top of the wall, so that it circulates continuously, creating a cool

micro-climate next to the building and reducing the heat gain through the glass. In short it is a water-cooled structure. Electric pumps do not, on the face of it, qualify as a 'passive' cooling device but these pumps are powered by the heat of the sun, converted to electricity by roof-mounted photovoltaic cells. Of course this only works during daylight hours, and some electricity has to come from the mains supply, but in an exhibition pavilion such as this the poetic idea of a cooling device directly powered by the heat of the sun is as important as the actual measurable performance.

On the roof of the building the cooling device takes the form of a series of elegant, double-curved, linear-fabric structures, raised up above the flat roof itself on V-shaped steel struts, 17. The whole assembly acts like a huge horizontal louvred shutter, casting a continuous shadow onto the surface of the roof below. This is essentially an air-cooled structure, preventing what would otherwise be a massive heat gain through the insulated lightweight roof deck. The louvres also support the photovoltaic cells providing the power for the water-wall pumps.

In Seville it is the afternoon and early evening sun that

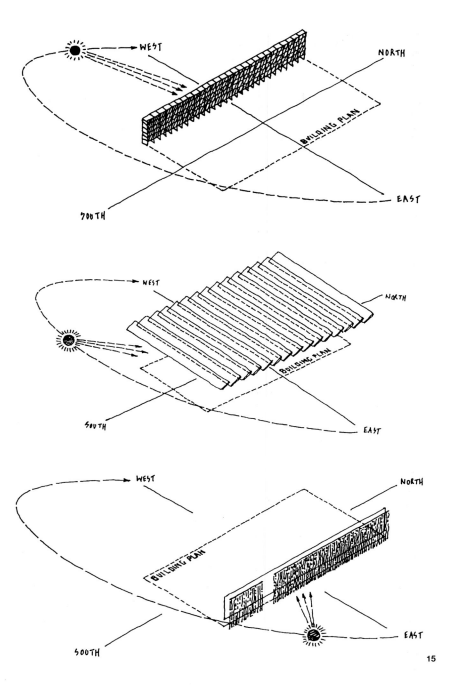

15

16

19

17

18

is hottest, so it is the west façade of the building that is most vulnerable to heat gain. Here the design makes use of a third, quite different cooling principle; not water cooling or air cooling, but cooling by sheer mass and thermal capacity. The principle has been described as that of the 'thermal flywheel'. The greater the mass of an enclosing structure the longer it takes to heat up and cool down. A lightweight wall will transmit heat directly to the interior of the building, quickly raising the air temperature to an uncomfortable level. But by the time a heavy wall has heated through, the sun has gone down and the heat from the wall radiates to the cool night sky. This is the principle that makes traditional heavy masonry structures effective temperature moderators in hot climates. They do not, however, lend themselves easily to the prefabricated, kit-of-parts building method favoured by Grimshaw. What was needed was a readily available heavy material that did not require to be crafted on site like a stone wall. That material, of course, was water. The only problem was how to contain it in a prefabricated structure. The answer was simply to make the wall out of a stack of water tanks, made from shipping containers, **18**.

The four-square, heavyweight structure of the west wall contrasts with the ultra-lightweight structures of the north and south walls. Here the basic material is not metal or glass, but a single layer of fabric stretched between bow-shaped masts. Cooling of the south elevation is achieved by external shading devices, again of fabric, which act like a tent fly sheet. These are attached in a louvre-like config-uration to the spreader struts which brace the masts, **19**.

The whole of the main envelope is thus conceived as a passive climate moderator. With the exception of the sun-powered water pumps, no energy consuming machinery is employed. Every cooling device is allowed its own architectural expression and nothing is concealed, so that the external character of the building derives solely from the climate-moderating technology. This is typical of Grimshaw's design philosophy which makes no distinction between technology and architecture. The energy conser-vation message is conveyed not by symbolism or gim-mickry, but by the purely functional components from which the building is assembled.

The effect of all these cooling devices is to reduce the temperature inside the building by up to 10°C on the

hottest days when the external air temperature can reach 45 degrees. But this is still above the level to which we are accustomed in modern buildings. And when a crowd of people is assembled in a relatively confined space, mechanical ventilation and cooling becomes a necessity. The enclosed pods are therefore air-conditioned in the conventional way. Mechanical plant is concentrated in three service towers on the west side of the building to allow continuous access for maintenance without disrupting the activities in the building. The outer two towers, opposite the two pods, are each flanked by slimmer towers of air-handling units. Horizontal air supply ducts, oval in section, emerge from the air-handling units just below pod level. The towers and the oval-section horizontal ducts are exposed to view, **20**, rather than being hidden away behind false walls or ceilings. Once again the climate-moderating technology, active this time rather than passive, is allowed its own architectural expression.

This, then, is the basic climate-moderating strategy. In the development of the design there has been some compromise and some dilution of the original idea of small air-conditioned enclosures within a larger, passively cooled envelope. At the competition stage it was envisaged that the natural 'stack effect' within the high main space would draw fresh air into the building through the lower part of the water wall. The air would thus be naturally cooled and humidified. But this idea had to be revised after detailed analysis when it became clear that the stack effect would be insufficiently strong and that in any case it was not wise to introduce humid air into the building on the hottest Seville days. It is also not quite true to say that the main space is cooled entirely by passive means. It is partly air-conditioned, benefitting from a limited direct air supply from the horizontal ducts as well as the overflow of conditioned air from the pod interiors. But this is an Expo pavilion. Its purpose is to demonstrate principles, suggest fresh approaches and to convey important messages.

Structure

In a British high-tech building nothing is ever faked. Everything is what it appears to be. What you see is what you get. In this building, therefore, the direct architectural expression of structure is as important as the expression of its climate-moderating function, and this means not just

23

making the components of the structure visible, but also making the method of their manufacture and assembly clear. It was always going to be a largely prefabricated structure, partly because of Grimshaw's fundamental belief in the advantages of industrial technology over site-based craft, and partly because of the opportunities that prefabrication offered to show off the manufacturing skills of British industry. It would be mainly a steel-framed, rather than a concrete or load-bearing masonry structure, because steel components could more easily be transported the thousand miles over land and sea from Britain to southern Spain.

But first there was the sub-structure to be considered. The Expo site is an alluvial flood plane in a bend of the Guadalquivir River. It has a low bearing capacity and almost every building on the site is founded on piles bearing on the firm substratum about 18 metres below the surface. In the case of the British Pavilion, these piles are of the 'driven, in situ' type, and were installed well in advance by a British subcontractor.

Early in the development of the design of the building it became clear that certain planning problems could most easily be solved by providing a lower ground floor to accommodate a bar and cafeteria, service areas like kitchens and toilets, and certain bulky items of mechanical plant such as transformers and chillers. The main concourse, just above ground level, is therefore a suspended floor, made from conventional in-situ concrete with columns and downstand beams. Above concourse level, however, the primary structure of the main envelope is assembled from lightweight steel components, prefabricated in Britain from mainly tubular steel by the well-known Warwickshire firm, Tubeworkers, **21**, **22**.

In principle, this superstructure is extremely simple. The box-like form, 65 metres long by 38 metres wide by 25 metres high, is supported by steel frames at 7.2 metre centres. Each frame consists of a pair of open lattice-trussed columns supporting roof trusses in the form of bow-shaped Warren girders, **23**, **24**, inverted to form a flat roof. The characteristic 'W' pattern of the struts was favoured by the designers over the more usual 'N' configuration because it simplified the welded joints, especially at the constricted ends of the trusses. It also gave the structure a lighter, less dense, visual quality. The trusses oversail the uprights to provide a shading canopy over the east and

24

west walls. Lateral stability is provided in the east–west direction by the uprights, which are cantilevered vertically from their fixings in the concrete sub-structure, and in the north–south direction by cross-bracing in the central bay only. The beams are fixed by means of pin joints rather than sliding connections. This has the advantage that the horizontal wind loads are shared between the uprights on either side, reducing the extent of their deflection, but it means that thermally-induced stresses have to be accommodated in the design of the girder. Continuous perforated universal column sections span horizontally over the tops of the girders to support the lightweight roof deck.

Each main frame arrived on site in four parts, the beams being halved for ease of transportation. Each half was first pinned to its upright and then lowered on the crane like a drawbridge, **25**, to be linked to its other half by means of a double pin connection. This assembly procedure is typical of British practice which favours factory, rather than site welding. All site connections are either pinned or bolted. In the early stages of the detailed structural design, a different, even more Meccano-like, fabrication and assembly strategy was considered, whereby the structure would be

broken down into its basic linear components of booms and struts, to be connected by cast steel nodes. These too would have been fabricated in Britain and shipped in containers, probably via the nearby port of Cadiz. The more distant port of Santander on the north coast offered more flexible handling facilities, however, and after checking the road route via Madrid for possible bottlenecks, the designers and fabricators decided that it was feasible to transport much larger components, up to 24 metres long and weighing up to 7.5 tonnes. This demanded a much higher degree of accuracy in the fabrication of the components, but it also speeded up the operations on site and produced a neater final result. This is a good example of the way the form of the building expresses not just the principles of the structure, but the method of construction and even the geographical relationship between factory and site.

Inside the main envelope, the pods have their own separate supporting structures. Visually they read as boxes, each one slung between four pairs of tubular steel columns. One might assume that they arrived on the site complete, to be lifted into place in one piece. In fact, however, they are simple platform structures and it is only

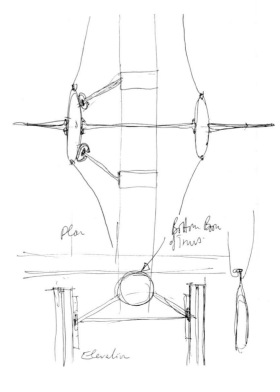

Left and opposite; extracts from Nicholas Grimshaw's sketch-books, dated 14 January 1989, illustrating the first stages of the pavilion's detailed development.

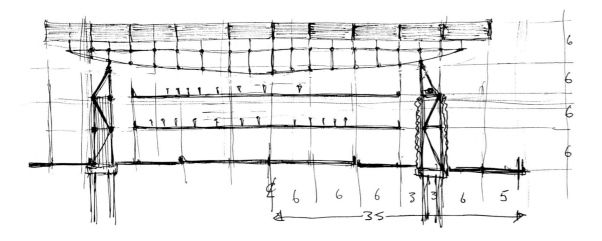

the curved metal cladding that gives them a pod-like appearance. Here for once the architectural form is not a clear expression of the method of construction. Roof and floor decks are each supported by a pair of warren girders, similar in form to the girders of the main envelope, **26**. These slot into the double columns, to which they are connected by 200mm diameter solid steel pins. The decks are of concrete, poured onto permanent steel shuttering spanning between the bottom flanges of universal beams.

Structurally the pods and platforms gain some lateral stability by being connected to the vertical frames of the main structure on the west side of the building. Visually, however, they read as separate, free-standing elements.

The third major structural element is the circulation system. This threads its way through the building from the main entrance bridge to the four external fire escape staircases via bridges and travelators linking the pods and platforms. Once again, it is a Meccano-like assembly of articulated components. Apart from the four ramped travelators (two up and two down) the main standard component is a steel-framed bridge based on a triangular section truss with V-shaped frames and tubular steel

booms and struts, **27**. There are only two different length versions of this standard bridge, spanning horizontally between the pods and platforms, and through the fabric external walls to the north and south escape staircases. Both the travelators and the bridges occupy the vertical slots of space between the pods and the east and west walls. They are suspended from the double columns of the pod and platform structures by means of elaborate outrigging assemblies of brackets and tension rods.

All of this steelwork of course needs to be fireproofed. Early consultations with the local authorities indicated that a three hour fire resistance would normally have been required for a building of this kind. This would effectively have ruled out exposed steelwork and undermined the whole concept of a prefabricated, bolt-together structure, clearly expressed. Ove Arup and Partners' fire specialists were able to argue, however, that the main fire risk areas were safely isolated in the enclosed pods. This, combined with the generous provision of sprinklers, smoke vents and escape routes, enabled them to reduce the required fire resistance to only half an hour for the main enclosing structure and one hour for the pods. This could be achieved by

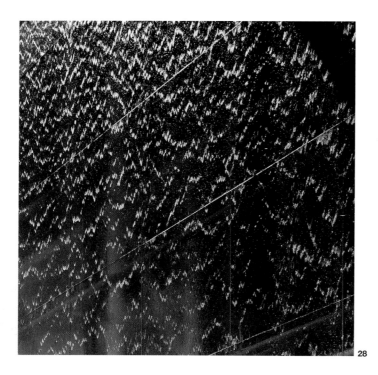

28

coating the steelwork in intumescent paint, applied in the factory and touched up on site after assembly.

External envelope

With the exception of the water-filled west wall, the enclosing envelope takes the form of thin membranes of various kinds, supported by lightweight secondary structures. The simplest and most conventional of these is the flat roof which consists of a single-layer PVC waterproof membrane laid on insulated troughed metal decking spanning between steel channel purlins. There are no falls, and no down pipes for rainwater. When standing water reaches a depth of 80mm it over-flows into gargoyles around the perimeter. Such a simple solution would certainly be considered risky in a more permanent building, especially since the membrane is punctured at regular intervals by the struts supporting the curved sunshades. It does however, offer an environmental benefit, the evaporation of standing water helping to cool the surface of the roof and reduce solar heat gain.

The most visible part of the external envelope is the water-cooled glass curtain wall which accounts for most of the east façade. Sheets are fixed together by means of internal steel spring plates bolted through the glass, and joints are sealed flush with silicon so that the whole wall is a single surface, with no projecting mullions or transoms to interrupt the flow of water, **28**. This is literally a curtain, hanging by tension wires from hockey-stick-shaped steel spigots attached to the raking tops of the main frame trussed columns. A series of horizontal aluminium extrusions, elliptical in section, apparently hover in mid air between the glass wall and the main frame. These are the key elements of the whole assembly, linking together the tension wires and spring plates, and connecting them to the structural steel. The architectural principle that demands the separate expression of every functioning element is thus carried through even in this small-scale secondary structure. This would be an impressively elegant and minimal curtain wall even without the cascade of water that covers its entire surface.

At 5 metres above the level of the pool, the wall is set back and supported by external glass fins. This allows the cascade to fall freely from its collection channel to form a curtain of closely spaced 'rods' of water. Visitors enter

29

30

32

31

through an opening in this curtain which is drawn aside by two curved projections from the collection channel. This water sculpture was designed by William Pye, who was also the specialist consultant for the whole water wall.

On the north and south ends of the building, the external membrane takes the form of panels of PVC-coated polyethylene sail fabric, fixed to circular hollow steel sections by means of continuous 'luff grooves' in exactly the same way that the sail of a yacht is fixed to its mast. The masts, at 4.0 metre centres, span the full height of the building and are attached at the top by means of sliding connections to accommodate any deflection of the roof beam, **29**. Such a large span would normally call for very heavy structural members, but these masts are only 324mm in diameter. The necessary stiffness is achieved by the bow-shaped profile and by tension wires, distanced off the main mullion by tapering pressed metal struts at 2.5 metre vertical intervals. The whole approach to the design of this secondary structure, including the actual materials and components, is thus borrowed from the boat building tradition – an example of the 'technology transfer' that is typical of Grimshaw's work. Yacht mast manufacturers

Proctor's helped with the development of the design, though the mast assemblies, each of which arrived on the site in one piece, were manufactured by Tubeworkers, **30**. The masts were engineered by Ove Arup and Partners' Lightweight Structures Group.

On the south elevation, further panels of fabric are fixed, louvre fashion, between the pressed metal struts to shade the main membrane and reduce solar heat gain. At the ends of the walls, and at the points where the pedestrian bridges pass through it to the external escape staircases, the fabric is carefully tailored and tensioned by an elaborate combination of luff grooves, clamping plates and elastic lacing to form a geometrically complex, but nevertheless neat and tidy watertight enclosure, **31**.

The detailed design of the water-filled west wall also borrows technology from outside the normal boundaries of the building industry. The original idea was to construct the wall from tanks of the Braithwaite type commonly used for water storage in industrial buildings, but these proved to be structurally inadequate and could not be stacked to the required height, **32**. The answer was to adapt the design of shipping containers, which were much stronger and could

34

fairly easily be made waterproof by means of a butyl rubber lining. The tanks are structurally independent units, 7.2 metres long, by 2.4 metres high, by 0.9 metres thick, with a mild steel frame and profiled steel walls, insulated internally with rigid non-hydroscopic foam. They are fixed together by marine twist lock connectors, with neoprene gasket seals, to form continuous walls, raised off the ground on open steel frames. These frames have their own foundations, but the walls are tied back to the vertical trusses of the main envelope frame for stability. No attempt is made to conceal these utilitarian, industrial structures, either externally or internally. As usual, the architectural expression is completely honest, **33**.

Two more elements complete the enclosing envelope. On the east and west elevations, the raking tops of the vertical main frame trusses are clad in insulated, double-skin GRP panels. Above these panels, clear polycarbonate louvres in aluminium frames fill in the gaps between the oversailing roof beams, **34**. The louvres provide outlets for exhaust air from the pavilion on the leeward side (a weather vane senses the wind direction) and also function as automatic smoke vents in case of fire.

Cladding of the internal pods takes the form of a wrap-around skin of corrugated aluminium on a metal sub-frame, with flat, riveted aluminium panels on the east and west ends. Both pods are completely lined internally and fitted out as audio visual theatres by the exhibition designers, Conran. A VIP reception suite has been constructed on top of the south pod. This has a curious hybrid structure, supported partly by the two main roof beams which pass over the pod, and partly by the pod itself. Tapered steel beams are threaded through the warren girders and supported by plates off the bottom boom. These support suspended ceilings, and provide lateral stability for partitions via sliding connections designed to accommodate a possible 30mm differential deflection between the warren girders and the pod structure. The curved bottom booms of the warren girders have to pass through the enclosed space, creating an awkward detailing problem. This is solved by wrapping them in transparent fabric stretched between luff grooves in tubular steel ceiling beams – an ingenious way to maintain the legibility of the structure and avoid unsightly collisions. The most visible part of the VIP enclosure is the perimeter glass wall, another exercise in

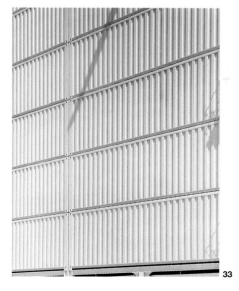

33

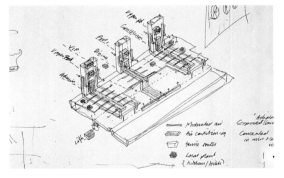

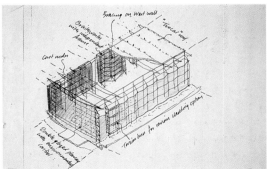

elegant framing with V-shaped pressed metal mullions and transoms, the mullions internal and the transoms external.

Conclusions

When the Department of Trade and Industry was searching for a suitable theme for the British Pavilion, it carried out a survey to find out how Spaniards viewed Britain as a nation. It soon became clear that in Spanish minds the mention of Britain conjured up images of tradition and conservatism, of gentlemen's clubs, country houses, parish churches and cricket on the village green. This was not an image of Britain that the DTI wished to promote. It seemed that news of the new enterprise culture of Britain in the 1980s had not yet reached Spain. The DTI determined therefore that it should present the image of a forward-looking industrial nation, skilled in science, technology, finance and communication. On the face of it, Grimshaw's uncompromisingly Modernist design for the pavilion supports this intention. And yet, in one sense, it is a traditional building. One might almost say that it draws its inspiration from Victorian buildings: not the revivalist architecture of Barry or Scott, but the engineering structures of Brunel and

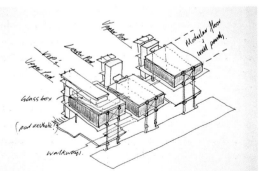

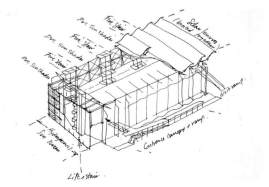

The project team's development sketches show the building with three free-standing 'pods' located within a simple enclosing envelope. Each 'pod', intended to contain special functions such as audio-visual theatres and performance spaces, plugs directly into a service tower on the western façade. As built, the pavilion contains only two pods located at the northern and southern ends of the building.

36 **37**

35

Stephenson. Most of all it stands in the tradition of that favourite of every British high-tech architect, Paxton's Crystal Palace, built to house the very first International Expo in 1851. In this sense, Grimshaw's pavilion is characteristically British: serious-minded, pragmatic and maintaining a faith in the industrial culture that nineteenth century Britain bequeathed to the world.

National symbols are not necessary to proclaim the Britishness of Grimshaw's pavilion. To an architect, if not to the average Spanish expo visitor, the large diaphanous Union Jack that hangs behind the water wall is superfluous. This is a functional building with a serious job to do. Some of the other pavilions have more instant appeal, but none display that characteristic British practicality. The pavilion on the adjacent site to the south, for example, is breathtakingly elegant, with its enormous painter's-palette-shaped suspended canopy and its fluid glass curtain wall. This is more like sculpture than architecture. Few would guess that it was the German pavilion, **35**.

But contradicting national stereotypes seems to be a common aim of pavilions at this Expo. Tadao Ando's Japanese pavilion is in this sense the opposite of the British pavilion. The Japanese seem to have concluded that their country's international image as a nation of high-tech workaholics needs to be balanced by reminders of its ancient traditions. Ando's monumental timber structure, **36**, **37**, is furnished not with electronic gadgetry but with religious images, beautifully crafted dioramas and displays of traditional crafts like origami.

Very few of the pavilions seem to have achieved a satisfactory balance between sensual display and serious content. The Finnish Pavilion is beautifully simple and well made, but seems too sober for a celebratory event like an Expo, **38**. The French is clever and daring, perhaps too daring. The original idea of a single skin of fabric stretched horizontally between four immensely strong columns has been lost but has proved a successful feature of the Palenque, **39**. Of the overtly symbolic and representational pavilions, only Imre Makovecz's Hungarian Pavilion achieves a seriousness to match Grimshaw's, and it does this by opposite means: natural materials, craftsmanship, organic forms and literal references like the doors in the shape of wings and the seven bell towers that pierce the upturned boat of the main enclosure, **40**.

38

39

40

The official theme of the Expo – Discovery – is not an easy one to express architecturally. The latest discoveries in genetic engineering, cosmological theory or artificial intelligence do not lend themselves easily to representation in built form. In comparison with the technologies of medicine, space travel and electronics the technology of building remains relatively primitive. Grimshaw's pavilion uses the most advanced building technology available, but its basic structure of prefabricated steelwork supporting an envelope of lightweight membranes, would be understood perfectly well by a Victorian engineer.

And yet, in one sense, this building does express the theme of discovery, for surely the greatest discovery of the 22 years since the last major Expo in Osaka is simply that the science and technology of modern Western culture – the culture that had its origins in the discoveries of the 15th century – is not the panacea for the World's ills that it was once thought to be. The official Expo theme may be discovery, but the unofficial theme of man's troubled relationship with the climate and ecology of the planet is the one that most accurately reflects global concerns at the end of the 20th century. The British Pavilion expresses these concerns most clearly. Because it is prefabricated, it is also potentially demountable and recyclable. The original competition report puts forward the idea that, when the building is dismantled, the solar powered pumps that drive the water wall might be combined with the storage tanks of the west wall to form water supply kits for the Third World.

Architects and architectural students all over the world are beginning to search for new ways to tackle the problems of pollution and resource depletion in building design. Low-energy climate moderation is an important item on this agenda, and here is a building that tackles that problem in a direct and practical way. There have been some necessary compromises in the basic idea of a passive climate-moderating envelope wrapped around air conditioned enclosures, but nevertheless the idea is powerfully expressed and suggests a future direction for the development of a new, green architecture. It would be an architecture that refuses to reject the ethos of science and technology, but instead redirects it to the solution of new problems. Like all the best experimental buildings in the 150 year Expo tradition, the British Pavilion at Expo 92 is an embodiment of the spirit of the age, **41**.

Night falls over La Barqueta Bridge; in the background are the masts and fabric roof of the Barqueta Gate, one of the principal entrances to the Expo from the city centre.

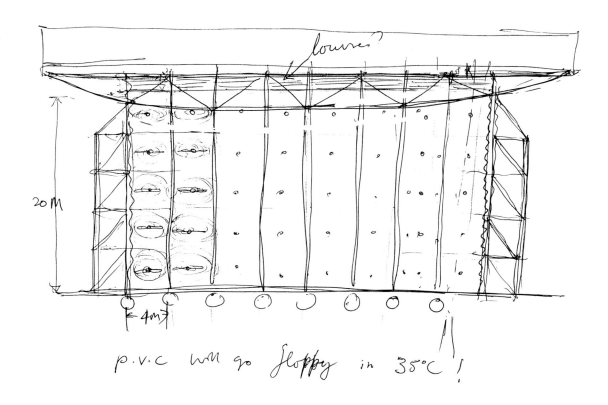

louvres?

20 M

4m

p.v.c will go floppy in 35°C!

One of Nicholas Grimshaw's first
sketch sections for the pavilion
from the sequence of sketches
dated 14 January 1989.

Opposite and previous page;
visitors enter the building
through a curtain of water which
is parted by two sculptural
curved projections designed
by William Pye.
Right; a fabric awning,
suspended from a tubular steel
structure protects queueing
visitors from the heat of the
Spanish sun.

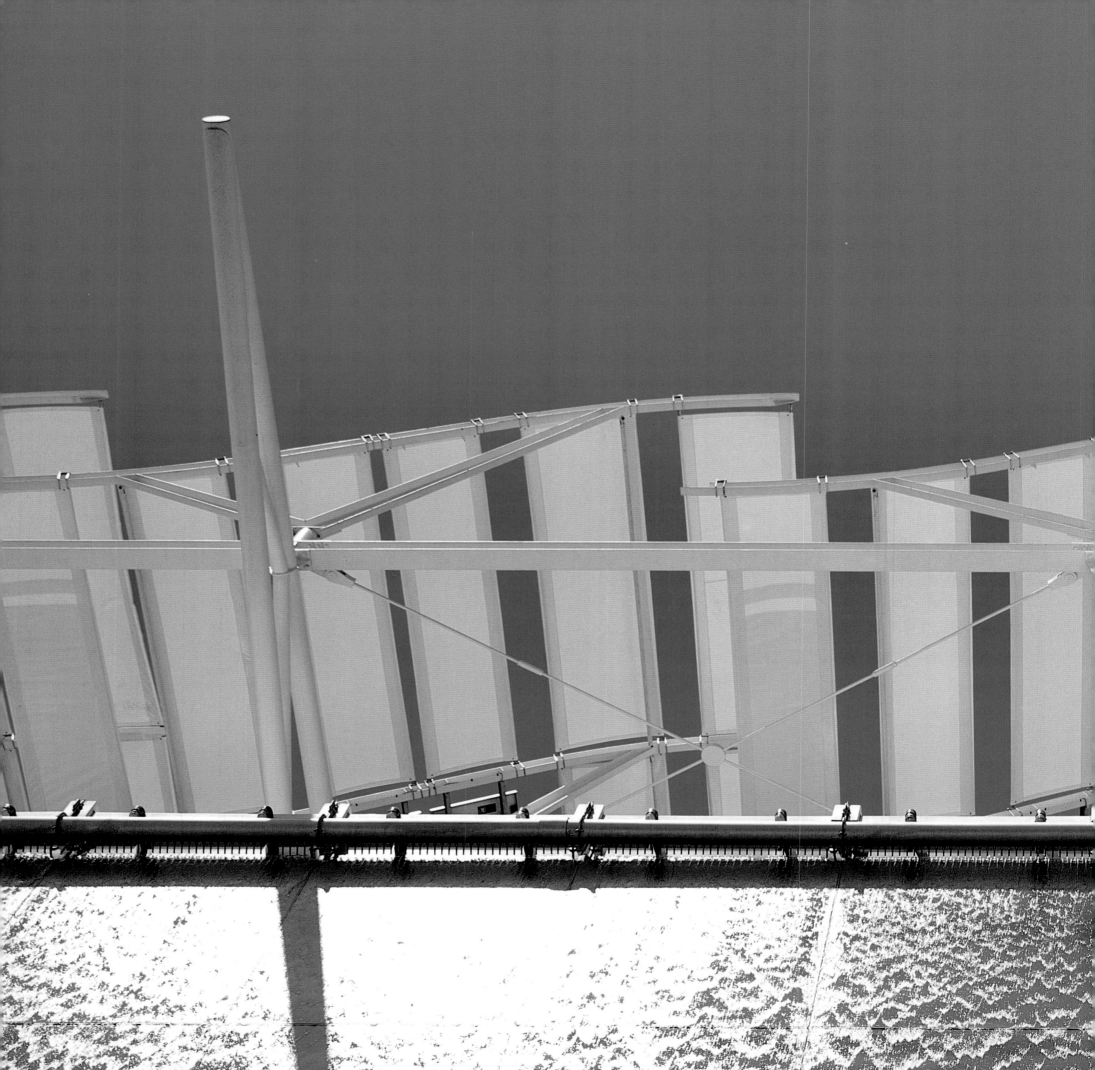

Previous page, left and right;
photo-voltaic cells mounted on
wave-like louvres on the roof
provide solar power for the
pavilion's water-wall pumps.

On the pavilion's south and north walls a single layer of fabric is stretched between bow-shaped masts; the south wall also carries external fabric shading attached in a louvre-like configuration to the spreader struts which brace the masts.

Detail of the junction of the water-wall with the fabric-covered north wall, left, and the south wall, right.

The fabric-covered south wall
carries additional sun shading
fabric louvres, some of which are
over-printed with fractured
elements of the Union Jack. The
fabric panels are anchored at the
corners to the spreader struts
bracing the masts.

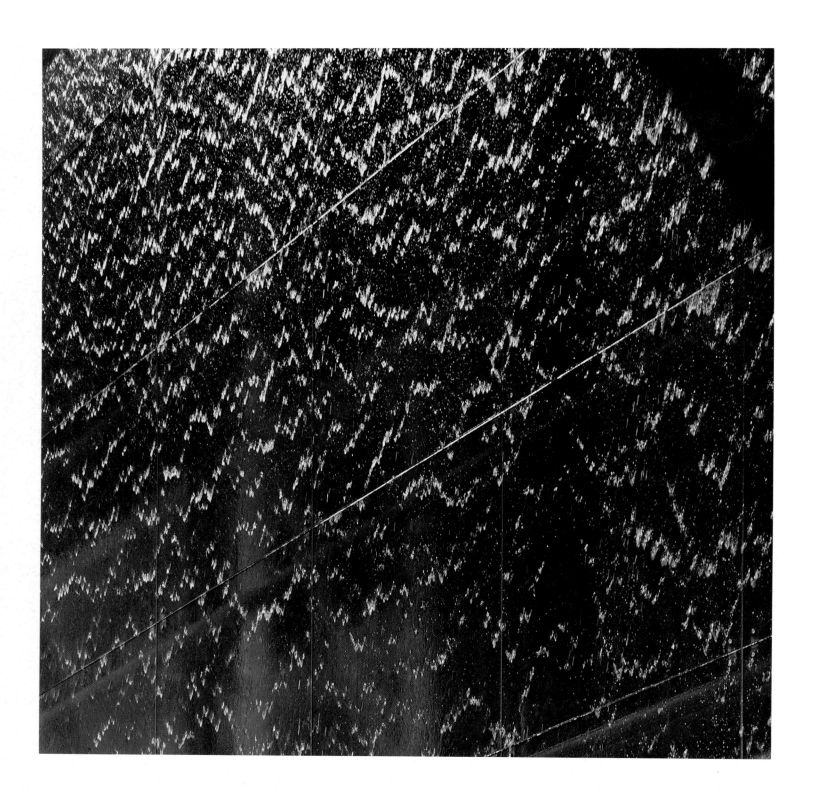

A sheer glass curtain wall, with
no projecting fixings, supports a
continuous sheet of water falling
into a pool, half inside and half
outside the pavilion.

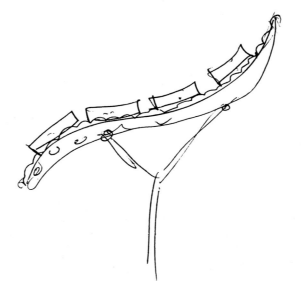

Far left; at night the building
becomes transparent, revealing
the framed structure supporting
the water-wall.
Above and left; roof top view
and Nicholas Grimshaw sketch
of the pavilion's wave-like sun-
shading louvres.

Within the pavilion's dominant, 'cathedral-like' space apparently free-standing accommodational 'pods' provide special spaces for audio-visual presentations and the like. Circulation between the pods and platforms is via a system of bridges and ramped travelators.

Perceptions of the water-wall change as one moves from outside the building to the interior. From within it appears crystalline and translucent, offering a partial and modulated view of the Expo activities.

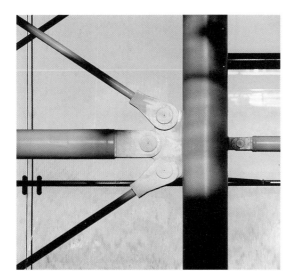

At a detailed level, Grimshaw's pavilion is as carefully crafted as any structure designed to last a lifetime. Paradoxically, this architectural and technological *tour-de-force* will have lasted only a single summer once Expo 92 has closed.

Location plan
1 UK Pavilion
2 Spanish Pavilion
3 river entrance
4 west gate
5 north gate
6 VIP entrance
7 service buildings
8 monorail
9 cable cars
10 parking
11 Monasterio Sta. Maria de las
Cuevas
12 station

0   100 metres
0   100 yards

old city

Pasarela de la Barqueta

Rio Guadalquivir

12

Puenta de
Chapina

lake

Pasarela de la Cartuja

9

Discovery Walk

2

5

8

avenue

European Avenue

avenue

avenue

3

11

1

International Avenue

7

4

6

10

Rio Guadalquivir

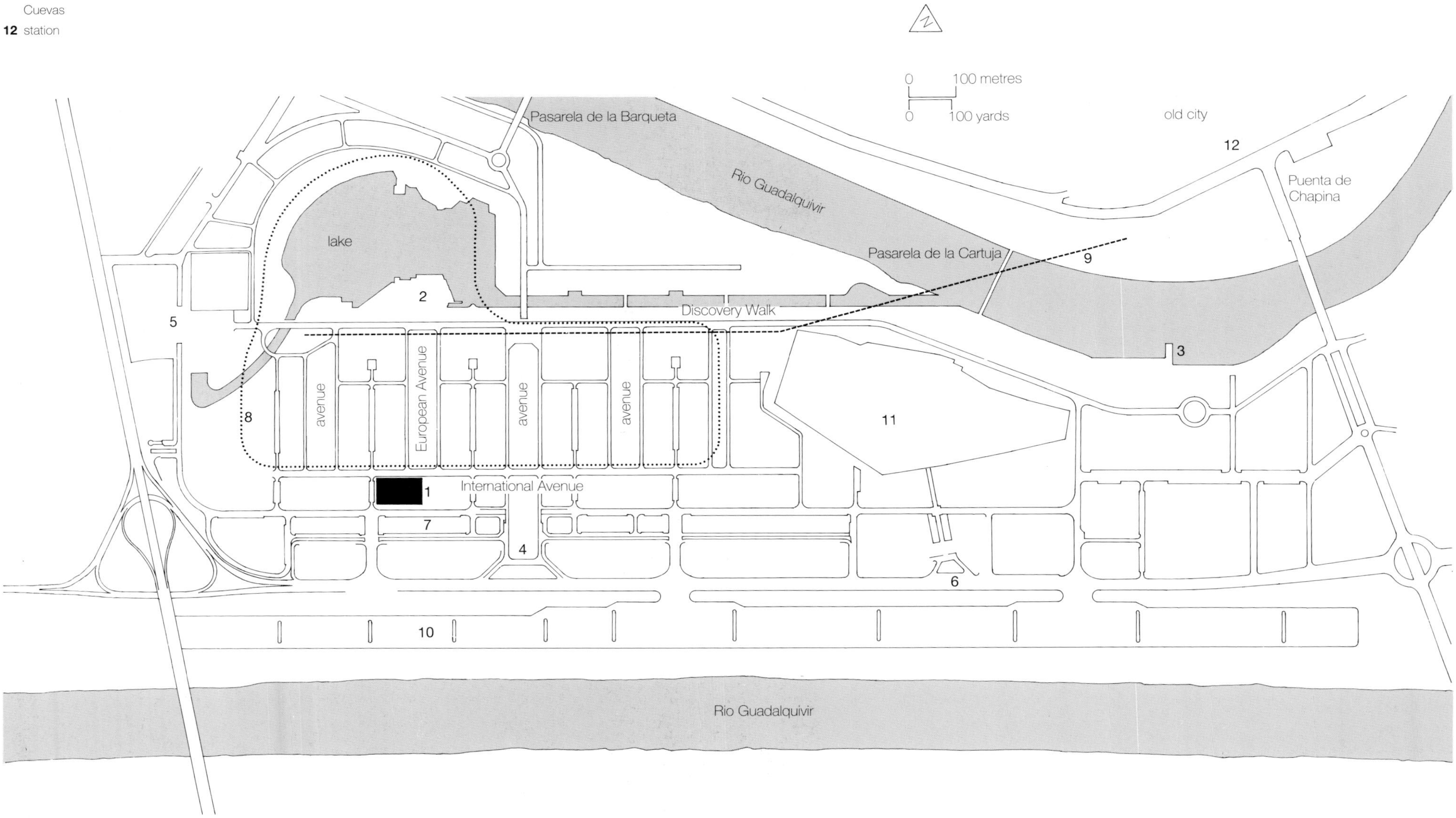

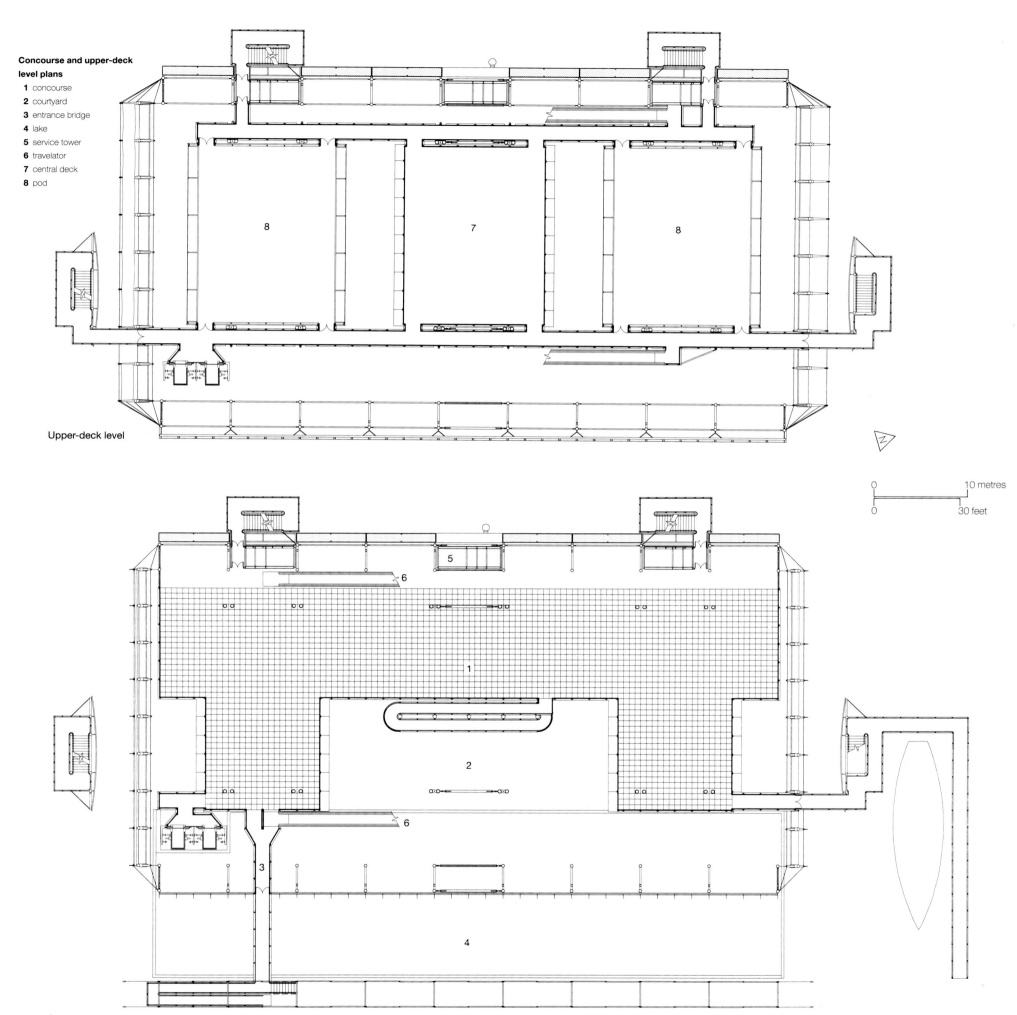

**Concourse and upper-deck
level plans**

1 concourse
2 courtyard
3 entrance bridge
4 lake
5 service tower
6 travelator
7 central deck
8 pod

Upper-deck level

Concourse level

0 _____ 10 metres
0 _____ 30 feet

Section east–west through

concourse

1 concourse

2 plant

3 courtyard

4 pod

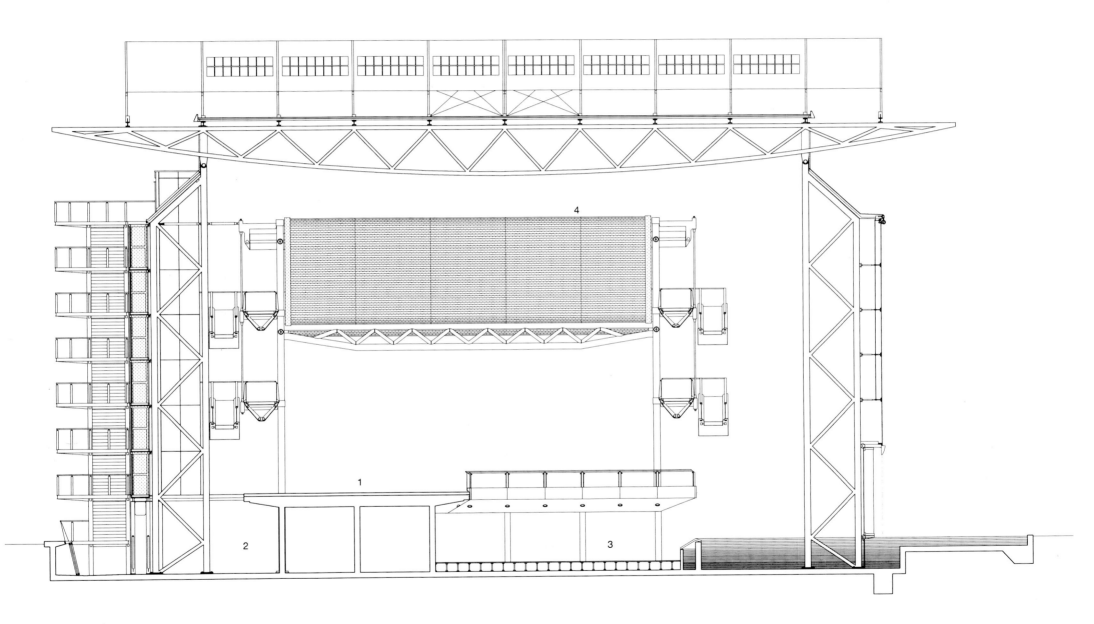

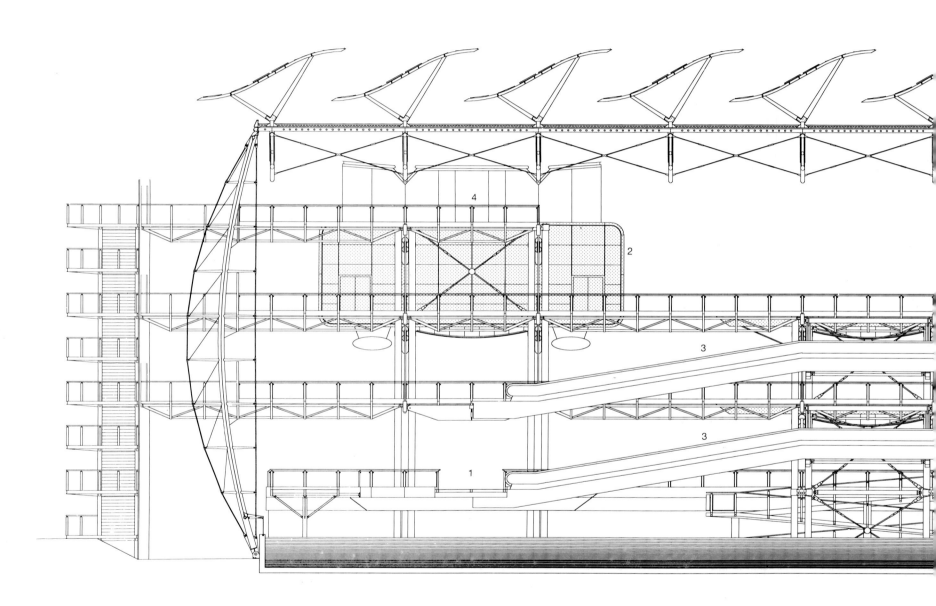

0   5 metres

0   15 feet

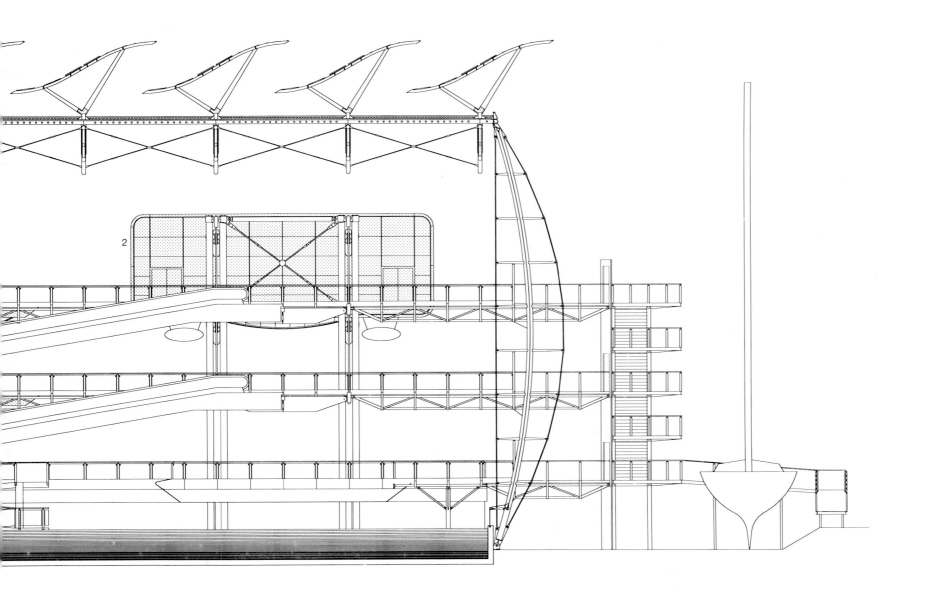

2

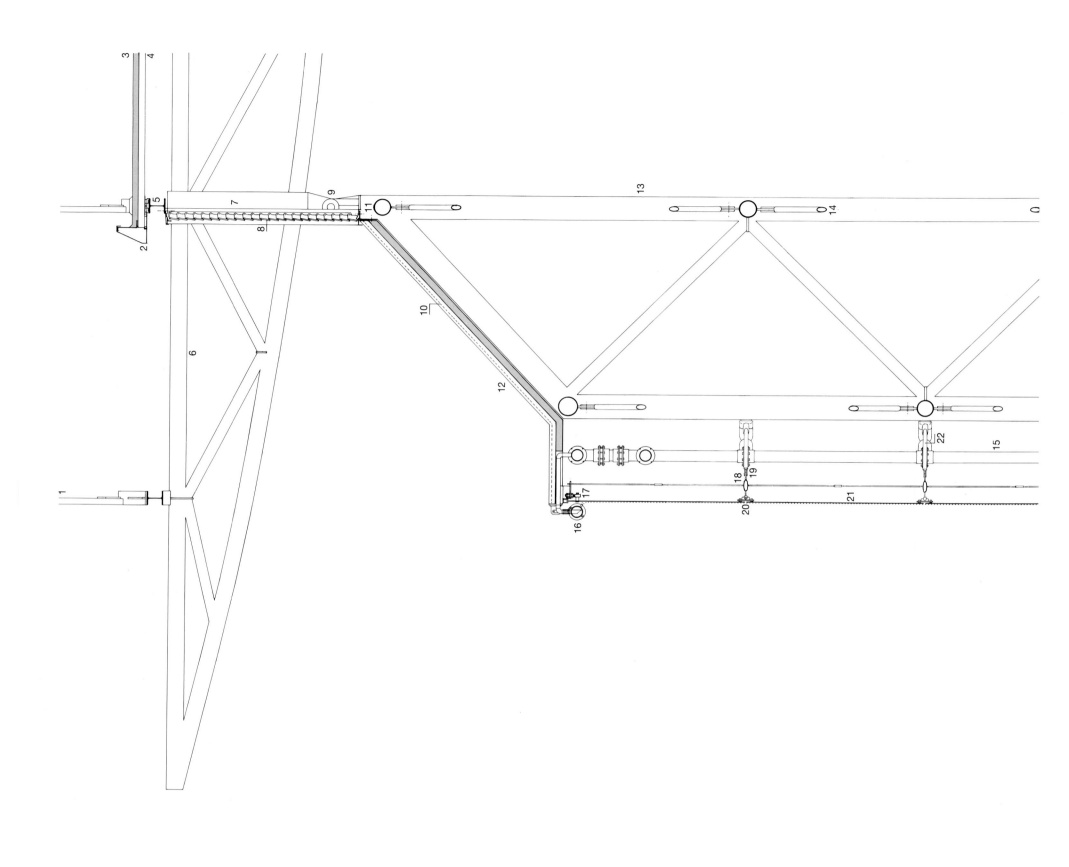

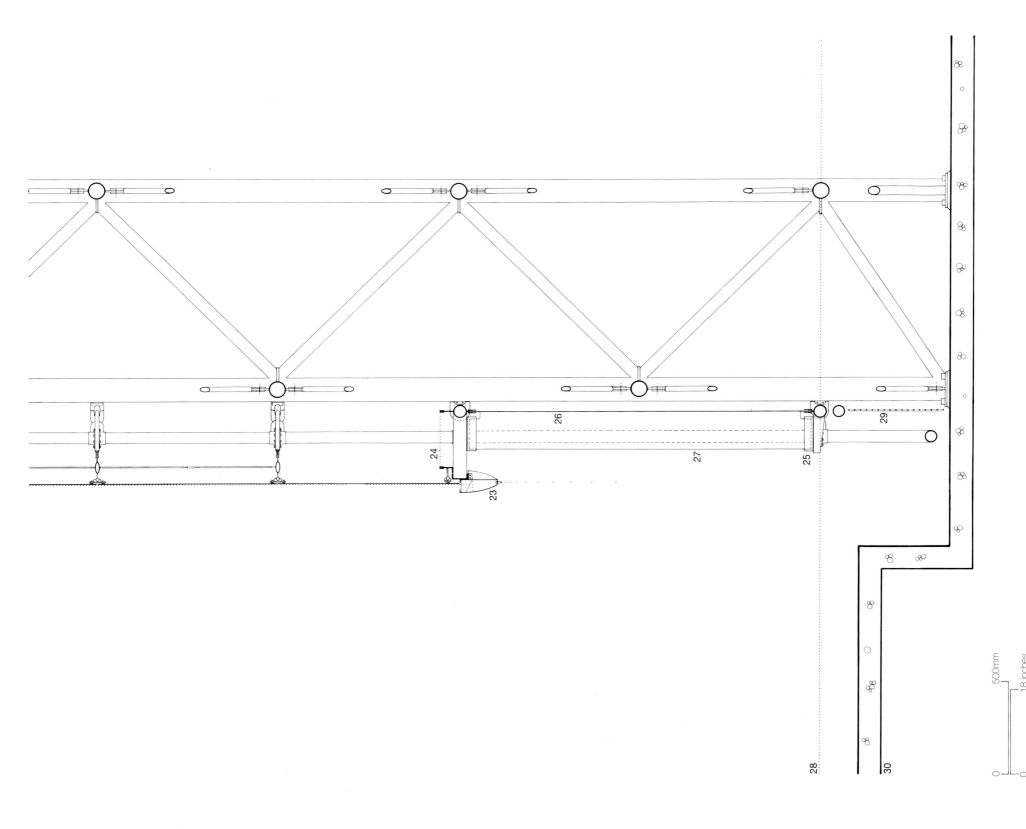

Detail section through east wall

1 solar canopy
2 aluminium coping and flashing PVF2 finish
3 membrane roofing on insulation
4 profiled steel roof deck
5 203 x 203mm universal column (UC) purlin
6 roof truss
7 steel plate at cladding interface
8 clear polycarbonate louvres in aluminium frame bolted to primary steelwork
9 pin connection between main roof truss and vertical truss
10 150 x 100mm rectangular hollow section (RHS) cladding rail pinned to primary steelwork
11 219mm diameter circular hollow section (CHS) cross member
12 insulated double-skin GRP cladding panel
13 vertical truss
14 CHS bracing in centre bay
15 180mm diameter ABS water supply riser supported off truss
16 150mm diameter ABS water delivery pipe in steel sling. Chemically welded joints at 1800 centres. Nozzles screwed into pipe at 50mm centres
17 forged steel glazing suspension pin fixed to steel cleat off cladding rail
18 aluminium transome suspended on stainless steel rod rigging
19 wind bracing assembly
20 glazing spring plate
21 12mm toughened glass with grey silicon joints
22 CHS strut connector
23 stainless steel gutter, outer surface mirror polished brass swivel nozzles fixed through base at 100mm centres
24 fabric soffit
25 mild steel glass fin base bracket bolted to RHS brackets
26 12mm clear float annealed glass panel in anodized aluminium section
27 15mm clear float annealed glass fin
28 water level
29 security mesh
30 300mm concrete slab

500mm

18 inches

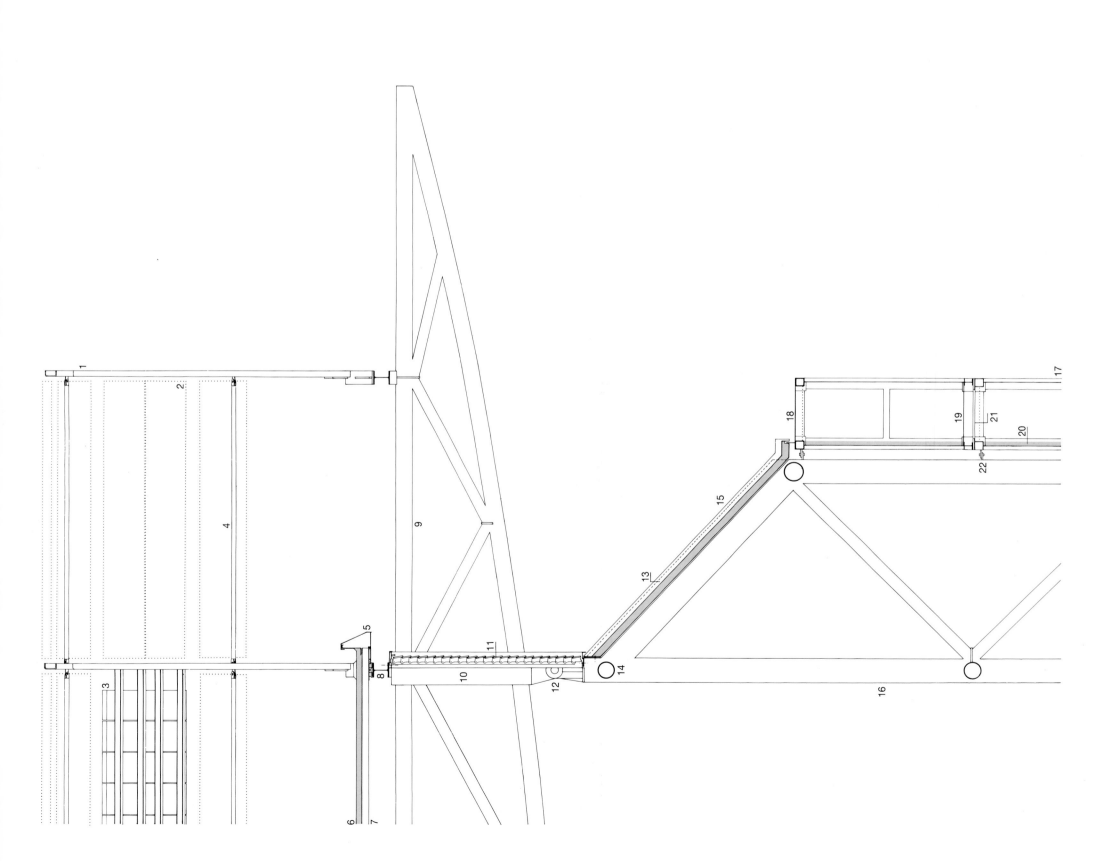

1 solar canopy: fabricated channel frame
2 solar canopy: fabric sun shades
3 solar canopy: solar cell modules supported between frames
4 48mm diameter CHS tie rail
5 aluminium coping and flashing PVF2 finish
6 PVC single ply membrane roofing on insulation
7 profiled steel roof deck
8 203 x 203mm universal column (UC) purlin
9 roof truss
10 steel plate at cladding interface
11 clear polycarbonate louvres in aluminium frame
12 pin connection between main roof truss and vertical truss
13 150 x 100mm rectangular hollow section cladding rail
14 219mm diameter cross member
15 insulated double-skin GRP cladding panel
16 vertical truss
17 water tank wall: profiled steel cladding on galvanized steel frame with factory-applied foam insulation and waterproof membrane. Tanks fixed together vertically by twist lock and block at each corner
18 galvanized steel chequer plate access deck
19 5mm steel plate tank floor
20 50mm rigid sheet non-hydroscopic foam insulation fixed to inside face
21 2mm galvanized mild steel panel fixed to top of tank
22 tank restraint brackets
23 metal grill on 125mm concrete slab on Holorib decking
24 152 x 89mm universal beam
25 tank wall support structure: 203 x 203mm UC with 114mm diameter CHS bracing
26 300mm concrete slab and retaining wall
27 fabricated tapered steel channel balustrade
28 taper cut channel fixed to concrete cantilever with heavy gauge metal grill between uprights
29 42mm diameter CHS rails
30 fibrous cement fire wall

500mm

18 inches

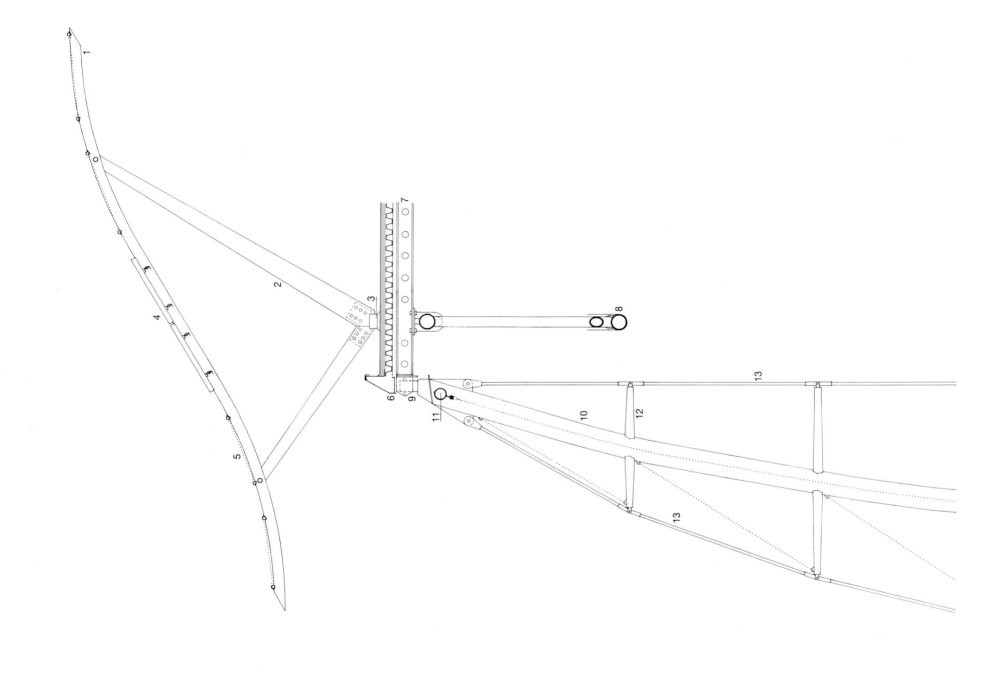

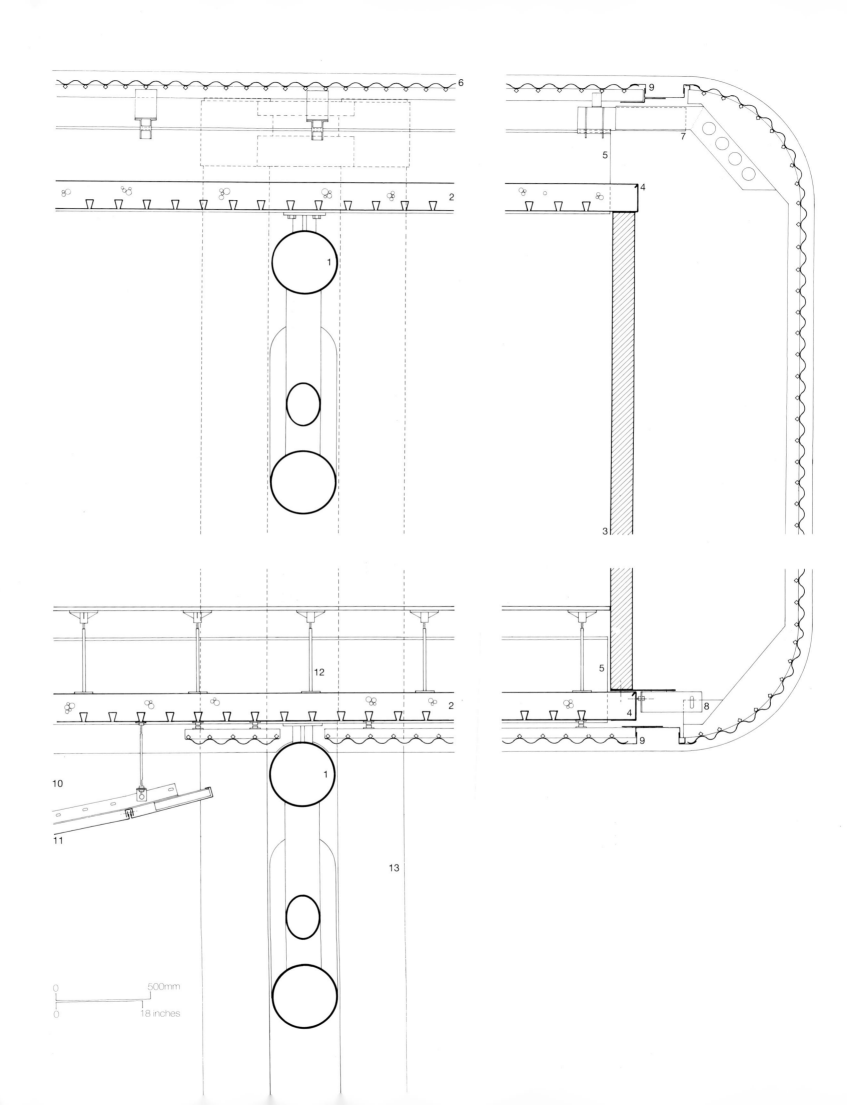

Detail section through pod

1 circular hollow section (CHS) primary support truss
2 acoustic enclosure: 150mm concrete slab on Holorib shuttering
3 120mm blockwork
4 150 x 150mm edge trim
5 457 x 191mm universal beam (UB)
6 sine wave profiled steel cladding planks clipped to fabricated channels
7 two-piece gantry bracket clamped to UB
8 sliding bearing connection permits +/-30mm vertical movement of either slab
9 service trough
10 service void
11 pressed steel panel underbelly suspended from Holorib soffit
12 raised floor
13 pod column

0 |_____| 500mm
0 |_____| 18 inches

Credits

Location
Seville, Spain

Client
Department of Trade & Industry

Architect
Nicholas Grimshaw & Partners Ltd

Principal Team Members
Nick Grimshaw, Mark Fisher,
Andrew Hall, Rosemary Latter,
John Martin, Christopher Nash,
Julian Scanlan, Rob Watson

Quantity Surveyor
Davis Langdon and Everest

Principal Team Members
Clyde Malby, Tim Gatehouse,
Andy Hewitt, David Connolly

**Structural and Environmental
Engineer**
Ove Arup & Partners

Principal Team Members
Richard Haryott, Ian Gardner,
David Hadden, Martin Hall, Tom
Harris, Brian Sherriff, Alain
Marcetteau, Nicos Peonides,
Chris Barber, Alistair Day, Rob
Harris, Sam Shemie, Peter
Berryman, Eric Budzisz, Jonathan
Cairns, Premini Hettierachchi,
Matthew King, Glen Mason,
Angus Moon

Management Contractors
Trafalgar House Construction
Management Ltd

Contractors & Suppliers

VIP Fit-out Designers: YRM
    Interiors
Exhibition Design: RSCG Conran
    Design Group Ltd
Water Feature Consultants:
    William Pye Partnership
Associated Architects: Exhibit,
    Seville
Modelmakers: Unit 22
Model Photography: Michael Dyer
    Associates
Excavation: Auxini, Seville
Piling: Simplex Piling Ltd
Concrete Substructure: Mivan
    Overseas Ltd
Concrete: McInerney España SA
Primary and Secondary
    Steelwork: Tubeworkers Ltd
Mechanical and Electrical
    Contractors:
    Rotary (International) Ltd
Lighting and Controls: Thorn
    Security Ltd
Lifts and Travolators: Otis
    Elevator plc
Solar Panels: BP Solar
    Systems Ltd
Electrical Switch Gear:
    Siemens SA
Roof: Texsa Ltd
Glazing: Briggs Amasco
    Curtainwall Ltd
West Tank Wall: Amalgamated
    Tanks International Ltd
Sail Walls: Proctor Masts Ltd
Fabric Structures: W.G. Lucas
    & Son Ltd
GRC and Plasterboard:
    B.R. Hodgson
GRP Cladding: Circle Industries
    (UK) plc
Smoke Vents: Greenwood Airvac
Internal Cladding and Concourse
    Floor: Environmental
    Technology Ltd
Metalwork: Architectural
    Metalwork
Flooring: Atlas Access Floors Ltd
Floor Finishes: Floorcraft
Water Wall Contractors:
    Thermelek Engineering
    Services Ltd
Water Feature Metalwork: Nitron
    Company
Abseilors: Technitube
External Works: Esereco SA

Detail section through typical access bridge

1 truss: circular hollow section (CHS) chords
2 cross plate
3 3mm rubber flooring bonded to 3mm steel plate
4 124mm deep purlins bolted to cleats welded to cross plate
5 PVC extrusion translucent white
6 3mm aluminium edge nosing polyester powder coated
7 perforated metal soffit with acoustic backing
8 service zone
9 circular light fitting in non-perforated metal soffit
10 Unistrut fixing for glazing between uprights
11 12mm toughened glass balustrade
12 strip luminaire
13 8mm mild steel (ms) formed channel upright polyester powder coated
14 50mm diameter ms handrail polyester powder coated
15 glazing fixing lug

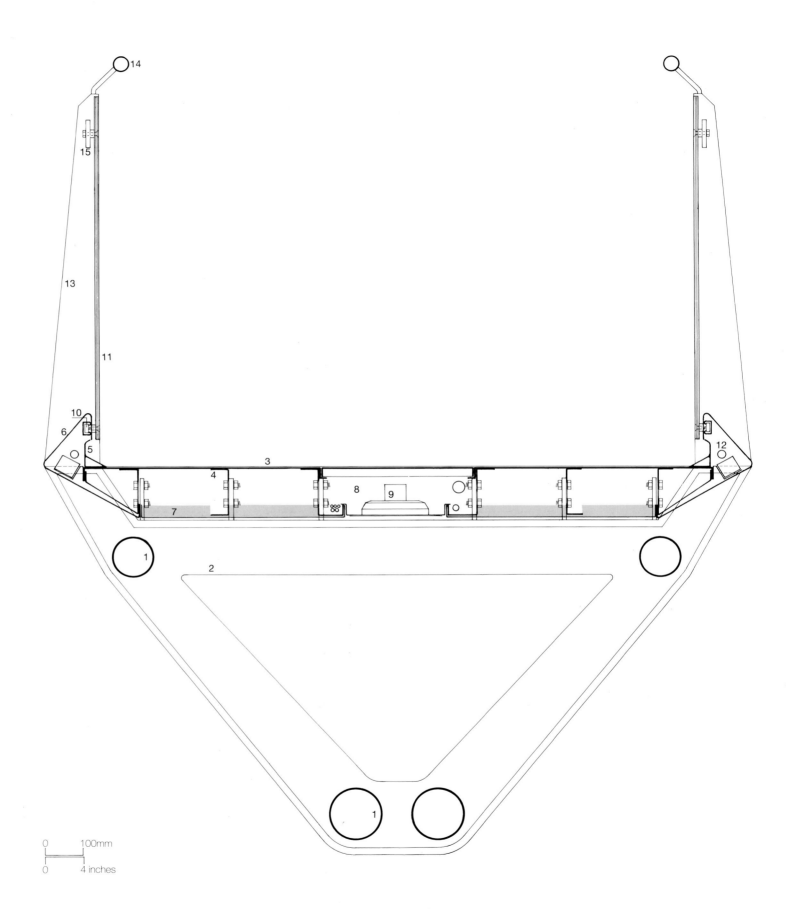

0   100mm

0   4 inches

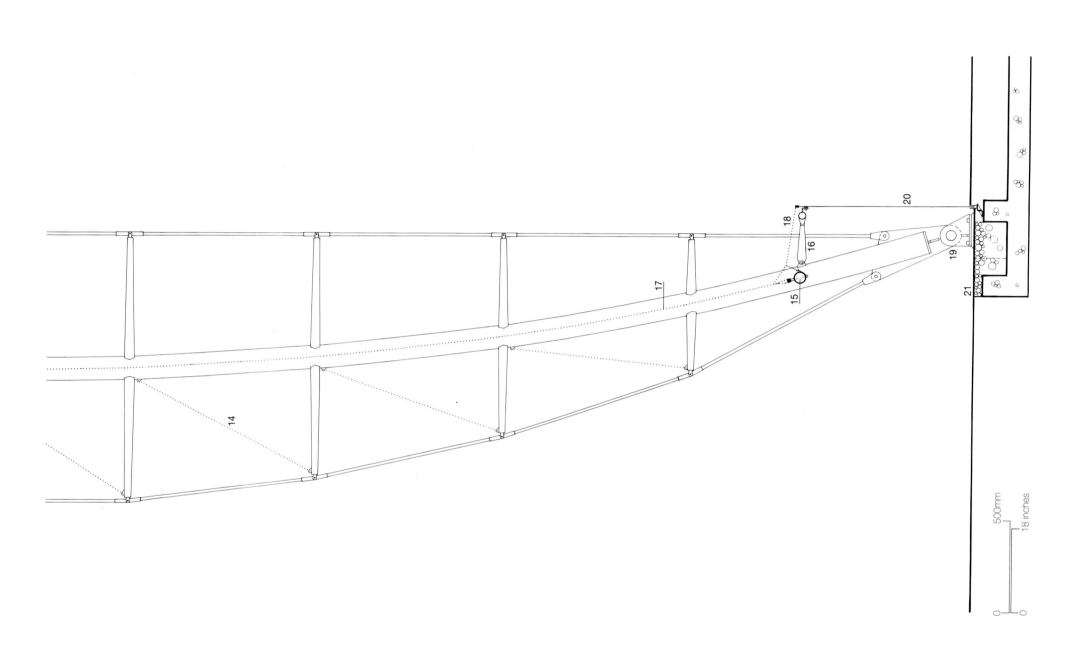

500mm

18 inches